# WINES WITH LONG NOSES

# WINES
## *with long noses*

by
### GEORGE BIJUR
&
### SIR HUGH CASSON

*London*
DENNIS DOBSON

Text first published in Great Britain in 1951
This edition first published in 1977 by
Dobson Books Ltd., 80 Kensington Church Street, London, W.8.
Printed in Great Britain by
Chelsea Printing Services, 186 Campden Hill Road, London, W8 7TH

ISBN 0 234 72003 4

Do you know which red wine Napoleon drank before every battle but one? How the laziness of a farmer's wife saved the vineyards of France? Which Bordeaux wine chateau was vainly offered, year after year, as a wedding gift to any engaged couple who would spend twelve months without quarreling? Why men-of-war lowered sail as they glided past Chateau Beychevelle? Which white Burgundy grows on the graveyard of a thousand wild horses?

The host who cannot paint for his guests the historical halo behind the bottle he is about to open, is missing half the pleasure of serving French wine. His dinner loses a conversational dimension—and he, an easy chance to enrich his raconteur reputation. He is tossing away an extra flavor—an imported, typically Gallic flavor that could inspire his listeners to keener appreciation, and permit even teetotallers to share the enjoyment of the wine.

Nearly every French wine, including *vin ordinaire*, brags a pedigree that Hollywood might easily transform into a movie-script. You have only to peer behind the label to glimpse adventurous ancestry worthy of the Bayeux tapestry—animated with the kidnapping of maidens, the glittering feats of knights in armor, the hot breath of that early flame-thrower, the dragon.

Back in the year 1520, Francois I's newly-appointed French ambassador to the far-off court of Suliman faced a precarious future. Previous emissaries had narrowly escaped being flung into the Sultan's torture-pit, where specially bred snakes and rats would slowly gnaw them alive. To minimize the risk of his giving indigestion to oriental rodents unaccustomed to French food, the new ambassador decided to bring the trigger-tempered sultan several propitiatory cases of wine from Chateau Carbonnieux, the Bordeaux vineyard whose 600-year-old, twin-towered castle still dominates the Valley of White Water. Jealous rivals in Francois' court mocked this unconventional gift. ''You must be crazy!'' they jeered. ''Don't you know that the Sultan is a devout Mohammedan, and would rather die than taste a drop of alcohol?'' But the ambassador was as stubborn as he was wily. Arriving at the land of minarets and dervishes, he had the bottles wrapped in silken embroidery and dispatched to the Sultan's Palace, accompanied by a tactful note begging His Highness to honor France by sampling her finest mineral water. Weeks later, the dread monarch and Defender of the Faith summoned the recently arrived Christian unbeliever. With haughty condescension he thanked the ambassador, but expressed bewilderment over a curious European custom. "I cannot understand why you French drink wine," he grumbled, "when your mineral water is so good."

The story has an unexpected sequel. Years later, a Barbary pirate kidnapped a beautiful but spirited barmaid from Bordeaux and presented her to the Sultan. At first her rages threw the entire harem into uproar. But gradually the mineral water's soothing effect calmed her nerves and she became the Sultan's favorite. Soon after, Benedictine monks of Sainte-Croix took over proprietorship of Chateau Carbonnieux. To fill the Sultan's increasingly large orders, France's leading interpreters of the Bible began to designate their wine in conformity with the Koran, and to label specially allocated shipments "mineral water of Carbonnieux".

Today Chateau Carbonnieux is one of the few Bordeaux vineyards to produce both white wines and red. The dry, neatly-nuanced white plays memorable flavor duets with oysters and trout. The suave red provides a connoisseur's way of wishing "Bon Voyage" to each mouthful of plump pheasant or crisp quail.

Like all wines of the region, Chateau Carbonnieux owes its flavor to a stony intruder that gives the district its name: Graves, from gravel. Gravel covers and studs the soil as thickly as raisins in a Christmas pudding. Gentler vegetables like string beans or peas, unable to

push their way through, fold up and wither. But the more muscular, more resolute vine, its roots clawing through the pebbles, benefits by exercise. When April showers dribble down or June thunderstorms drench, the crackling gravel serves both as faucet and filter. It permits just the right amount of moisture to seep through to refresh the vine roots. Thus, in its slow way, it literally transforms water into wine.

Also in Graves, ten minutes by jeep from huge concrete pens where Nazi submarines lay in wait for night attacks on Allied convoys, Chateau Haut-Brion presides over a small army of skilled laborers, among whom the most punctual, talented and indispensable is an unpaid, overtime worker; the sun.

Haut-Brion's reputation dates back farther than Tudor antiques. When the Pilgrim fathers sailed from Plymouth, British nobility were already paying the fabulous price of 2500 pounds sterling for a *tonneau* (about 900 bottles). With such enormous gusto did 18th century hosts rely on this wine to rhapsodize a roast, and with such obstinacy did they refuse to slake their thirst with any other, that at auctions from 1750 until the French Revolution, clamorous bids for Chateau Haut-Brion drove auctioneers hoarse and so soared its prices that a *tonneau* consistently fetched 500 pounds more than the next *cru*.

In 1801, Talleyrand remarked "The power of speech was given man so he could disguise his thoughts." Soon after, grooming his cellars for the Congress of Vienna, he left no cork unturned in his search for a wine whose

coaxing bouquet and disarming mildness would enable him to infiltrate the defenses of rival diplomats, peek through their camouflage and fathom their plots. Never a man for half-measures, once convinced Chateau Haut-Brion would make the ideal secret weapon, he wasted little time fiddling around in the purchase of random casks. Instead, he bought the whole chateau.

Any Irishman named O'Brien who visits France today will find to his exasperation that everyone, from immigration control officer scrutinizing his passport to room-clerk scanning his signature, will pronounce his name "Haut-Brion". Historians are inclined to bet this same phonetic fate befell the vineyard's original owner: that he was an Irishman who, eventually weary of protesting "My name is pronounced Haut-Brion, but I spell it O-B-R-I-E-N", surrendered and adopted the French spelling. Proof remains blurred, but today's owner is an American who seldom fails to wear a shamrock on St. Patrick's Day.

On the opposite side of the highway wiggling west to Arcachon where shepherds patrol the moors on stilts and watch over sheep hidden in shoulder-high grass, stands Chateau La Mission-Haut-Brion, a surprise package in stone. "Why it's just like an iceberg," drawled a youthful naval lieutenant, recently arrived from Reykjavik. "It pokes down deeper underground with its cellars than up in the air with its towers." Across the ceiling of its venerable chapel, now a museum for wine relics, all the great vintage years for centuries past are dazzlingly inscribed in jewelled letters. Beneath

this planetarium of claret constellations looms a statue of the mysterious patron saint of wine throughout France, St. Vincent.

Not even the Sorbonne's oldest, whitest-whiskered professor can explain how St. Vincent originally acquired this heavy, perennial responsibility. A fourth century deacon at Saragossa, Spanish crossroads town halfway between the Pyrenees and Madrid, he was martyred at Valencia. But the gold and scarlet, hand-illuminated parchments of that period contain not a word suggesting he ever drank wine. Why then did vintners pass over so many more celebrated saints, with greater seniority and greater influence, with halos bigger than flying saucers and brighter than neon lights, to settle on an obscure junior? And why did the French, always fervently nationalistic, choose for the extra-important job of heavenly wine-watchman, a saint who had spent his life in Spain?

Abbé Krau, the exuberant curate of Vosne-Romanée in Burgundy, and an etymological detective able to give lessons to Sherlock Holmes, has evolved an ingenious theory. "C'est très simple" the curé will remark, while absent-mindedly searching for the spectacles posed on his nose. "It's because the first syllable of 'Vincent' forms the word, vin. He's the only saint whose name is half wine."

But it was St. Vincent's post-Paradise activity, Bordeaux' wartime mayor used to explain to Allied destroyer commanders, which gave name to the banquet wine they were sipping with such relish. It seems that

one autumn afternoon when grapes were being plucked in the fields of Graves, *le bon dieu* felt that St. Vincent, his sommelier and wine adviser, needed a refresher course in the latest terrestrial vintages. So He stamped a visa, good for sixty days on earth, on St. Vincent's passport, and parachuted him to France, entrusted with this top-secret mission. During his inspection tour the celestial visitor strolled over to Pessac. The wines he tasted there seemed so incomparable, so heady, so overwhelming that he forgot the road back to Heaven and established La Mission-Haut-Brion.

When the French film "Monsieur Vincent", winner of many awards, played at Bordeaux recently, the cellar-master of Chateau La Mission-Haut-Brion saw it five times. That was because he believed in a more mundane paternity for his chateau and because the film's hero, acted by Pierre Fresnay, was Vincent de Paul—the 16th century ascetic who first succeeded in making charity fashionable.

After having been captured by Barbary pirates, sold as slave to a Turkish fisherman, and escaped back to Bordeaux, the young prelate entered the home of Count de Joigny as tutor to his nine-year-old son. From then on, mounting higher and higher on the national tide-wave of religious renaissance, Vincent persuaded the rich and the noble to help the hitherto despised sick and poverty-stricken — persuaded dainty countesses in powdered wigs, pearl necklaces and rustling satin gowns, to visit foul-smelling slums as "servants of the poor", and even to nurse lepers. So impressed was the Queen,

Anne of Austria, that she established a monastery at Pessac for Vincent's Preachers of the Mission. Their task was to arouse throughout France the same compassion for the unfortunate that Vincent had awakened at court. Since, like most monasteries, La Mission-Haut-Brion had to rely on vineyards for income, its brothers were compelled to allocate their zeal equally between the vine and the divine. Throughout the Middle Ages, its wines went solely to religious dignitaries. "Could you possibly manage to get me a cask of La Mission-Haut-Brion?", prince and marquis would plead with their archbishop. Contributions to the Church nudged noticeably upward.

Gradually the vineyard's production expanded, and a few lay notables were permitted to purchase. Among them was Marshal Richelieu, nephew of the great Cardinal, and an Army commander under both Louis XIV and XV. Reproached occasionally for his inability to stop quaffing goblet after goblet of the velvety claret, he used to reply: "If God did not approve of drinking, why would He have made this wine so good?"

A ten minute hop by helicopter from Pessac northwards through the wine-vaporous clouds hovering over Bordeaux would land you in St. Julien, heart of Haut-Médoc, where waits that most photogenic of chateaux, Beychevelle. To far-off dinner parties it wafts not only a deep red claret whose scented flavor flirts enticingly with your palate, but also a troubador's repertory of anecdote.

When Henri III, son of the crafty, conspicuously ugly Italian orphan, Catherine de Medici, mounted the throne, his character teemed with enough contradictions to puzzle a psychiatrist. Tall as a guardsman, slender as an Olympic athlete, he drenched himself several times daily in perfume, and dangled so many bracelets and necklaces that, with each movement, he tinkled like a Balinese bell dancer. Sometimes, for special court occasions, he would dress in women's clothes.

Disdaining logic, the king chose a non-sailor, the Duke of Epernon, wealthiest noble of Guyenne and owner of enormous feudal estates including lush St. Julien vineyards, to be his Grand Admiral. Henceforth, each boat tacking across the Gironde estuary on its foamy way from Bordeaux to the sea was obliged, as it passed the Admiral's river-side chateau and vineyard, to dip sails in deferential salute. Gascon *patois*, the *patois* of Cyrano de Bergerac, soon altered the oft-heard command "*Baissez les voiles!*" ("lower the sails"), to Beychevelle.

With age, the King's eccentricities turned to violence. They climaxed in his treacherous assassination, at the Chateau of Blois, of the people's favorite, the Duke of Guise and his brother, Cardinal of Guise. Horrified and furious, France rocked with resentment. A Dominican monk, Jacques Clément, reckless of fate in this world, but deeply concerned for the next, trudged from theologian to theologian, inquiring, "If I kill a king who has slaughtered the flower of the Church, will my soul survive?" Reassured, the black-cloaked friar crept by the royal guards, hid in an ante-chamber, and exultantly stabbed Henri III to death.

After the king's dead cousin, Henri of Navarre, first of France's Bourbon monarchs, was crowned Henri IV, his tactful reign brought peace and prosperity. Aided by an energetic Prime Minister, Sully, he drained marshes, helped farmers, introduced silk weaving, developed the making of wine bottles and glasses, built the Pont Neuf and the Gallery of the Louvre, completed the Tuileries, constructed highways and flanked them with poplars.

The Duke of Epernon shared the general good fortune. His honors became amphibious. Retaining the post of Grand Admiral, he was also appointed Colonel General of the Army. His St. Julien wine, relished by the king, became revered by the people. Few homes could afford Beychevelle, but all could and did copy Henri IV's favorite sauce, the silky yellow fluff which today's *garçon* solicitously spoons alongside your *chateaubriant* or *entrecôte*—and which 16th century chefs promptly christened *sauce béarnaise*, after the province of Béarn where the king had been born.

As Henri IV become grayer, his subjects nicknamed him "The Green Gallant" (*le Vert Galant*). He had collected some sixty mistresses of authenticated status and public notice—thus recapturing for a delighted France the international record which seventy years earlier had been carried off by Henry VIII of England.

After Henri's assassination, as the King was riding with Epernon by his side in an open carriage, the Regency passed to his widow, pudgy, blonde Marie de Medici.

For her banquet table, Beychevelle's owner devised a novel wine receptacle called a *nef*, a miniature sailing vessel on wheels, its crow's nest and superstructure crenellated like the battlements of a castle. In its spacious cabin, the Queen could lock up her favorite bottle. If she wanted to show favor to a visiting prince, she would give the *nef* a brisk shove, rolling it down the table until opposite his place. To call added attention to her gesture, with each turn of its wheels, the *nef* emitted a shrill whistle.

Since Marie's tyrannical, sixteen year old son, Louis XIII, instinctively distrusted his father's favorites, Epernon was banished and his family dispoiled of his estates. Yet if you examine a chateau-bottled Beychevelle today, you will see that homage is still being rendered to the medieval admiral—not only in the Médoc's nautical name, but its heraldry. Across the label is blazoned a gargoyle-prowed caravel, its mainsail dutifully curtseying to the deck.

Formerly the owl-infested woods and firefly-illumined marshes encircling Chateau Beychevelle were said to be haunted by bearded witches, three-legged goblins, were-wolves and women in white. On Mardi Gras, they assembled for a spirited Walpurgis Night dance directed by a demoniacal master of ceremonies named Leonard. Today, yielding to mechanisation and the Marshall Plan, all the spirits except one have disappeared. The castle, whose triangular towers seem to sketch gray witches' hats on the pale blue sky, is still haunted by a lady ghost, always wearing white and always dressed in the

latest Parisian mode. This proves, say vintners, that Beychevelle's bouquet is so alluring, so distinctive, so powerfully pervasive, that it wafts its appeal all the way up to Heaven and all the way down to Hell, calling all gourmets, including ghosts, with the irresistible, come-hither magnetism of the Lorelei crooning into an inter-planetary loud-speaker.

A wine that often swirls in Lalique glasses at diplomatic dinners is suave Chateau Lafite-Rothschild, noted for its almond-like flavor and a faint scent of violets. For such a wine, which billows its aroma across the room so you can detect the perfume as you open the door, the French have coined an amusing epithet. "It has the long nose," they say, transferring the olfactory organ from the sniffer to the sniffed.

A lesser-known *cru* also notable for its fragrance, is Chateau Cantemerle. Neighbor of the great Chateau-Margaux, for whose aristocratic red wines Countess Dubarry used to send a coach 500 miles from Versailles, Cantemerle's legends could fill a slow-playing phono-graph record.

The literal translation of Cantemerle is "Sing, black-bird". But why should such a name be bestowed on a vineyard? You can choose between two explana-tions, equally curious. Puffing at his pipe, the scholarly master of Cantemerle will tell you there was once a horrible dragon which ravaged the whole countryside of Haut-Médoc—a dragon bigger than the Loch Ness mon-ster and with scaly hide thicker than the armor of a Sherman tank. Growling with insatiable hunger, the dragon devoured the countryside's rabbits, fox, sheep, and deer—and took special delight in blackbirds for dessert. A handsome knight, his name too complicated to set in type, galloped up the Médoc, fought on foot with the monster for three days and nights, and finally slashed off the dragon's fire-breathing head. All the blackbirds of Bordeaux then flew to Macau, assembling in the sky like squadrons of Spitfires on D-Day. Hailing their liberator with a mass serenade, this triumphal twittering gave the chateau its name.

For the second version of Cantemerle's origin, the scene shifts to the Hundred Years' War. After the British invaded Guyenne, ancient province whose capital was Bordeaux, their troops achieved victory after victory until they penetrated to Macau. The local French seigneur could muster only a few hundred men-at-arms and three cannon to defend his castle, but he proved himself a tactician worthy of Eisenhower's staff.

Concealing his inadequate artillery in the adjacent forest of Souves, he ordered his chefs to serve an epicurean feast to the enemy archers. Slaughtering his calves and trundling down from the smoke-room his tangiest hams, this military Machiavelli made sure each dish was liberally sprinkled with salt. Then he paraded forth his heftiest two-handled banquet goblets, brim-filled with potent red wine.

When the commander saw the English had become tipsy, and heard a few significant snores, he shouted the cryptic order: "Chante, merle!" The biggest of his

hidden cannon, nicknamed "blackbird", because of its dark, bird-breasted barrel, hurled a booming charge of grapeshot into the enemy. Surprised and befuddled, they surrendered.

When an extra-smooth wine trickles down your throat, leaving the palate purring with warmth, French wine growers describe this ecstatic sensation by a picturesque phrase: "C'est le bon Dieu qui descend en culottes de velours." ("It's the Good Lord sliding down your throat in velvet pants.") Often this is altered to "C'est le Christ qui descend en culottes de soie." ("It's the Lord Christ gliding down in pants of silk.") Neither phrase implies the slightest sacrilege: they merely reflect the naive, peasant imagery that inspired pickaninnies in Marc Connelly's "Green Pastures" to conceive of the Lord as smoking huge black cigars.

A claret that often provokes this imaginative praise is Chateau Talbot, whose vineyards lie only a few minutes from Chateau Beychevelle. How, you may wonder, did a French vineyard ever acquire so British a name? In London, certain Piccadilly restaurants strive to make an impression by the mere typographic device of printing *le* or *la* before even the most commonplace dishes on their menus: "Le kippered herring", "La pudding de Yorkshire", "Les potted shrimps". But in France, where even the taxi-driver scorns John Bull's meagre cooking and volubly sympathises with Englishmen condemned to lives of culinary martyrdom, no vineyard proprietor would ever borrow a British name. Here is how it happened.

During the same Hundred Years' War in which Cantemerle's wine triumphed over English arrows, John Talbot, ex-governor of Ireland, proved the most dashing British commander and stoutest adversary of Joan of Arc. As a reward for defeating the Burgundians and saving Normandy, King Henry VI, pious, studious founder of Eton—for "twenty-five poor and needy scholars to learn grammar"—bestowed on Talbot the counties of Shrewsbury and Wexford in England; and across the Channel, the St. Julien vineyards of the Marquis d'Aux. Talbot reciprocated by keeping the English court liberally supplied with huge oaken casks of his wine. Henry's Queen, Margaret of Anjou, called it "nectar of the beautiful and of lovers".

When the French besieged Castillon, stronghold of Britain's Gascon allies, the veteran Talbot, now Earl of Shrewsbury, rushed to the relief. Without waiting for artillery, he attacked the enemy's strongly fortified camp. Leading his army of archers in dogged charges right into the fire of French artillery, Talbot was killed, and his body so disfigured that next day his own herald found it difficult to recognize.

Although thousands of Frenchmen perished under the fury of Talbot's assaults, his enthusiasm for Bordeaux vintages has subsequently caused all to be forgiven and endowed his name with the lustre of a regional, if not a national hero. "He killed more Frenchmen than the plague," Médoc vintners remark philosophically, "but he taught British princesses to appreciate French wine."

In a land where nude statues wear not fig-leaves, but

*wine*-leaves—where the season's most spectacular beach costume, Balmain's Bikini bathing-slip, is fashioned from plastic green wine-leaves—there could be no warmer praise.

Nearly 500 years before university glee clubs first warbled "My Darling Clementine", Rabelais had scribbled love songs in praise of his darling *vin clémentin*. Now as then this tulip-toned claret comes from Chateau Pape-Clément, the only Bordeaux vineyard whose vines have ever been personally trellised, pruned and harvested by a Pope.

In the 13th century, a young canon, Bertrand de Goth, who could out-argue any priest in Graves and out-wrestle any blacksmith, inherited manor and vineyards from his uncle, Archbishop of Bordeaux. Throwing himself into the study of grapes with the same fervor he had devoted to the scriptures, his vinicultural improvements caused the wine's reputation to soar. But his tenure as vineyard superintendent was short.

When Pope Benoit XI met violent death in 1304, just after his predecessor had suffered a similar fate, the terrified College of Cardinals found difficulty electing a successor. They chose Bertrand, who had meanwhile risen to Archbishop. After he became Pope, assuming the name of Clément V, the armies of three states menaced the papal palace. Refusing to be bullied, he moved the papal court from turbulent Rome to the security of Avignon. Occasionally he returned to Pessac and found relaxation by puttering, clipper in one hand, trowel in the other, among the vines.

Often he deplored the lack of fidelity in marriage and the disturbing lack of harmony among human beings. "I'd give everything I own," he used to say, "to find just one couple who did not quarrel."

In his will, he left his vineyards to the archbishops of Bordeaux—and for 500 years Gascon gossip insisted that any affianced couple who could pass twelve months without quarreling or repenting their engagement, could demand the vineyard of Chateau Pape-Clément as wedding gift. But at the Revolution's outbreak in 1789, the archbishops of Bordeaux were still waiting for the first such idyllic couple to come and claim their reward.

At St. Emilion, whose purplish red vintages earn an asterisk of honor on carefully drawn wine-lists, you can visit the world's one and only church with a restaurant perched upon its roof. After the Moors swarmed up from Africa and set fire to French villages, a hermit whose name has been variously written Aemilianus, Innilionus, and Emilion, trudged through the devastated towns to meditate in the peaceful forest of Combes. Enrolling in the abbey of Saintonge, he was assigned the daily baking of bread. One morning some young novices, seeking relief in practical jokes from the monastic humdrum of their lives, hid the long-handled hoe with which Emilion used to poke the loaves. Uncomplaining, he crawled into the flaming furnace and arranged the loaves with his bare hands. When he emerged without having singed an eyelash, he was hailed as a saint.

Years later he left the abbey and spread his straw pallet on the bare rock, inside a cavern some twenty miles east of Bordeaux. Other Dominican monks, drawn by his fame, plodded many dusty miles from remote villages in France and Spain to share his meditation. Dwelling as cave-men in the grotto's darkness, they chipped away the stone until, after 300 years of patient labor, the enlarged cavern was finally shaped into St. Emilion's great underground church, hand-hewn from a single rock.

Wine is not the town's only speciality. It can list two others: macaroons and marriages. Here macaroons have been liberated. Here they are not tethered to the ice-cream plate, but allowed to scamper all over the menu and all around the clock. Eight p.m. at the beer-garden-style restaurant atop the monolith church sees macaroons occasionally accompanying the consomme, always escort-ing raw apples, pears, bananas—and frequently disguised in melted cheese. Eight a.m. at any local hotel . . . macaroons greet you for breakfast.

Deep down inside the cavern, only a few steps from St. Emilion's stone couch, bubbles a crystalline spring whose pin-filled basin attracts husband-hunting young ladies in wholesale quantities. Water-clocks as in the Pincio Garden at Rome, water-driven puppet theatres as at Schonbrunn, water-propelled fireboats—these are no longer unique, but this subterranean spring is perhaps Europe's only water-driven fortune teller, specializing in the prediction of matrimonial destinies. Every year on St. Emilion's day, girls of all ages queue before the basin. Into the shimmering water, each aspirant tosses two pins. If the pins fall athwart one another,

as if for a Scottish sword dance, then the lucky girl who threw them can be certain that within a year wedding bells will proclaim her marriage.

As your Citroen slithers up a winding hill from the monolith church to the vineyards, bumps in the roadway make the car leap and buck like an enraged rodeo bronco. In a curious way the unevenness of these cobblestones provides a tangible proof of the wine's perennial popularity.

When Henry VIII's British courtiers tasted St. Emilion, it was a case of love at first sip. Demand grew so great that ships leaving Bordeaux for the Thames, used to carry an entire cargo of oak barrels fire-marked by St. Emilion guilds and filled with their wine. On the return trip, the crews would load cobblestones as ballast and then, docking in the Dordogne's muddy estuary, heave the blocks ashore. The thrifty French immediately carted the stones to St. Emilion—and thus, cobble by cobble, the vineyard road was paved.

British working men and Bordeaux vineyards have one thing in common: tradition bequeaths to both the right to a courtesy title not generally used in other regions. In Britain, the courtesy title, "Esq.", follows a man's name; in Bordeaux, the courtesy title of "Chateau" precedes a vineyard's name.

In Bordeaux the list of wine-growing properties automatically assuming the impressive title, "Chateau", is enormously varied. Even though the vineyard is the region's shabbiest, even though the owner's house is no more elaborate than Pocohontas' wigwam, even though

no building at all rises from the premises—such material chateau shortage in the inventory inhibits the wine label no more than would the lack of a regiment cramp the style of a Kentucky Colonel.

In Burgundy, tradition veers in exactly the opposite direction. The vineyard may be fronted by a castle twice the size of Versailles, yet the title "Chateau" will almost never appear in the name. The vineyard of Clos de Vougeot, for example, boasts a magnificent feudal chateau, complete with three gilded gates, chapel, and banquet hall to seat 900 guests. But its wine remains simply "Clos de Vougeot" (clos, meaning "enclosure, vineyard").

In this sprawling mansion, once a monastery, the ermine-robed Chevaliers du Tastevin now stage their candle-lit wine tastings. Behind the revelry, lies a strange conflict. As painted oak rafters echo to the tinkle of guitar and the minstrel chant of Francois Villon's drinking songs, an architectural war wages perpetually between rooms strikingly mismated. The decorative clash, incongruous as a debutante wearing a fencer's mask with evening gown, is no accident. It harks back to a medieval drama of pride and punishment.

When the white-haired abbé of Citeaux decided the monastery needed bigger quarters, he commissioned a young monk who had studied architecture in Italy to draw up plans. Months later, the friar, on the crest of creative enthusiasm, brought the designs to the abbé's bare-walled cell. Excitedly, he explained the dotted lines, pointed out advantages in the vaulted ceiling, the buttressed roof, the brighter light that would sift through glass windows stained with vegetable dye. But as the old man peered at the parchment sketches and listened, his fingers began to drum restlessly on the table and his habitually kind expression darkened to a frown. Without waiting for the young monk to finish, he reached out his arm and swept up the sketches. "My son, you have grievously erred," he thundered. "In your zeal, you have committed the deadly sin of pride. To punish you, and save your soul, I shall turn these designs over to other monks, instructing them to add the most monstrous errors they can conceive. All their blunders will be built into the monastery—but your name will go down in history as its architect."

Although the abbé may have succeeded in stamping out pride, the vineyard supervisors of Clos de Vougeot have ranked among Europe's most arrogant men. Confident and aloof, supremely certain of the rarity of their wine, they have not hesitated to tell conquering generals and victorious emperors to go chase themselves. The Almanach Bourgignon describes how Napoleon, the day after his sensational defeat of the Austrian army at Marengo, when he was at the very height of his popularity in France, let it be known he would like to celebrate by drinking some venerable Clos de Vougeot with his dinner. The answer was not long in coming. "If he wants to taste Vougeot forty years old," gruffly announced Dom Goblez, keeper of the monastery's cellars, "let him come here and drink it. We're not selling any."

Fifty years later a Colonel named Bisson whose other

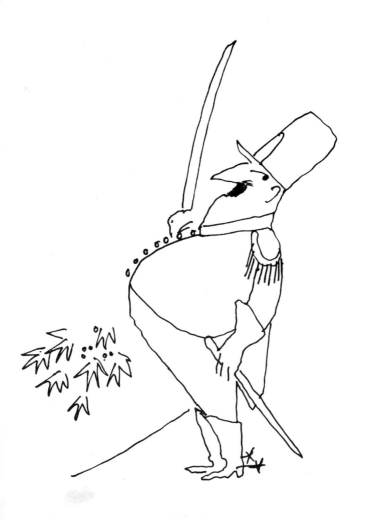

military exploits have been forgotten, rendered himself immortal—at least in Burgundy—by figuratively tearing up the manual of arms and inaugurating a new salute. His troops were tramping wearily home from the eastern front where they'd been engaged with the Prussians. On the dusty road to Dijon, they marched by the green slopes of Clos de Vougeot. "Reg-i-ment halt!" the colonel suddenly barked. "Pre-sent arms!" Whirling on his heel, he snapped his sword upright almost touching his face, while his troops stiffly raised their muskets, rendering to the vines the reverent homage due to a Commander-in-Chief.

If legend can be believed, Clos de Vougeot has done wonders to prevent divorce. "What do you think of my vineyards?" the Duke of Burgundy is reported to have asked a peasant's pretty wife, a lass named Perrine. "Oh, sir, they're lovely." "And how do you like the wine of Clos de Vougeot?" "Oh, sir, I like it very much," she murmured with eyes demurely downcast, "especially when it's my husband who drinks it."

If you were to send a Rolls-Bentley complete with leopard skin linings, twenty-four carat gold door-locks, and motor-cycle escort to fetch dinner guests, you would scarcely be paying them a more flattering compliment than to serve Corton—for by that gesture, you treat them as Emperors. After Charlemagne's drive against the Moors, climaxing with Roland's death at Roncevaux, his peace treaty with Caliph Haroun-Al-Raschid, hero of the "Arabian Nights", brought to France gifts of ivory camels that danced on their hind legs, mechanical

nightingales trilling Arab melodies, gigantic elephants in jewelled silks—and secured for all Christians forlorn ruins of Sainte Andoche-de-Saulie, sacked by the Saracens. Distressed by this infidel affront, the emperor donated sixty acres of his own family property to provide funds for rebuilding the church. Ever since, wine from these secluded Corton vineyards, where trespassing goats were condemned to lose their tongues, has been known as the "wine of Charlemagne".

Corton's list of royal customers has lengthened with passage of time. Its red-crowned bottles nestle in the cellars of kings-in-reign George VI of England, Haakon VII of Norway, Frederick IX of Denmark—and kings-in-reserve Leopold III of Belgium, and Peter II of Yugoslavia.

In Burgundy's wine nobility one of Corton's few peers is Chambertin, the wine which Napoleon usually carried in his knapsack. The little Corsican, stoutly maintain the city fathers of Beaune, would never have lost the Battle of Waterloo if his orderly had not forgotten, the night before, to tuck a bottle in his saddle-bag. Wellington's batman, with unfair and diabolically stolid British dependability, remembered to serve *his* master the accustomed port.

Chambertin is perhaps the only wine in the world whose production doubled because of the delightful sound of its name. And it all happened because Charlemagne's mother was named Berthe. After her son's stratospheric rise, mothers throughout France hastened to christen their daughters Berthe and their sons Bertin, in the optimistic hope that duplication of name would

mean repetition of career. Among the many Bertin's that would have been listed in a 12th century census, was a farmer whose land bordered the scattered vineyards of the Abbey of Bèze. Envying the monastery's success with wine, Bertin decided to plant his own fields with the same grape—the Pinot. Soon not even the monks could distinguish between the flavor of their wine and his. To their dismay, the upstart wine from *Champs de Bertin* (literally, "Bertin's field") grew not only just as well-known as Clos de Bèze, but even took the lead. Visiting wine-buyers found the name "Chambertin" more sonorous, more rhythmic, richer in promise. So the pioneer vintners of Clos de Bèze, practical men with an early understanding of advertising, decided to abandon their original brand-name and market their wine also as Chambertin, a custom which has continued ever since.

Pouilly Fuissé, the *cru* that is exported to England and the U.S. more often than any other white Burgundy, owes its beguiling flavor to the carniverous appetite of a vanished race of troglodyte cowboys. Its vineyards, sheltered in a vast bowl between the twin villages of Pouilly and Fuissé, sprawl in the shadow of a jagged cliff, La Roche de Solutré, roughly twice as high as the Leaning Tower of Pisa. About 5000 B.C., the region was invaded by a wandering tribe of cave-dwellers who particularly fancied horse-meat. Since primitive bow and arrow had not yet developed their much later ability to knock down swift prey at long range, the tribal hunters ingeniously relied on the cliff as

secret weapon. Shouting and shrieking, they'd encircle a herd of wild horses and stampede them uphill, then race behind until the cornered, panic-stricken animals, finding no other escape, would plunge off the precipice to equine suicide. Thousands of such prehistoric skeletons, unearthed by archaeologists at the cliff's base, have impregnated the soil with a buried treasure of calcium nuggets constituting the fabulous equivalent, if appraised as vine-nourishment, of a richly loded Yukon goldfield. Little did the hunters know they were putting gold in them thar hills, or at least depositing pounds-sterling and dollar bills and thousand-franc notes in the bank accounts of future owners. In all the world's history, few other hunting grounds from the Pytchley in Northamptonshire to Nairobi in Kenya have seen each square foot of land skyrocket so spectacularly in value—and merely from being hunted over.

As your highway twists west in Burgundy, and your Michelin road-map shrinks the Spanish border to a thumb's length away, you hear tales of the passionate ardor that Julius Caesar displayed for bullfighting—and his acrobatic handling of the lance when mounted on horseback as picador. Half a day's gallop from an amphitheatre where Caesar used to joust, doze the sloping vineyards of Moulin à Vent.

The gaunt windmill ("*moulin à vent*") that tops this Beaujolais ridge gives the impression of a giant black rooster, angrily flapping tattered wings. More effective as scarecrow than to grind grain, it nevertheless has

much to crow about. It proclaims the spot Caesar chose as rest-camp, immediately after his conquest of Gaul, and has been declared a national monument by the French Government, ranking with the Arc de Triomphe and Notre Dame.

After his army had broken speed records in their forced marches, Caesar explored the country north of Lyon, seeking a spot where his weary soldiers might regain their energies and his wounded recover their health. When he finally discovered a valley where both the wheat and the wine were abundant, he established his garrison, and stayed so long that today village children, making mud-pies in the backyard, often stub their toes on a centurion's rusty helmet. To this peaceful camp, Caesar gave the name Romana-Esca ("Roman nourishment"), altered by time to Romanèche, the village where you now pull up to inspect the vineyards of Moulin à Vent. Here the grape is the Gamay—and the garnet wine offers the economical advantage—common to its Beaujolais country cousins, Fleurie and Juliénas—that the fruity flavor is already delectable when only six months old, without requiring years of aging that swell the price. Under the inspiration of this wine, Caesar wrote many chapters of his seven-volume war commentary—including the "Gallia est omnis divisa in partes tres" Latin chore whose laborious memorizing often causes prep school lads to miss their favorite television.

Not many husbands hoist themselves to fame on the silken rope of a wife's laziness. But at Romanèche-Thorin, the pensive statue of Benoit Raclet and the torch-lit October festival when gaily garbed peasant girls swarm from other villages to dance in his honor, prove it can be done.

Back in Marie Antoinette's day, French vineyards shivered in peril before a plague of luminescent, butterfly-hatching, fire-worms, the *pyrale*, whose voraciousness threatened to exterminate the vines as utterly as Biblical locusts had destroyed the grain of the Egyptians.

What to do? Town criers in big cities and tiny hamlets jangled bells and summoned wise men to meetings where their blended learning might compound a cure. Astrologists recommended spells, to be read on nights when Scorpion was in ascendancy. Barbers proposed leeches. Alchemists and apothecaries, furiously disputing how many grains of diamond dust should be ground into insect powder, shouted unprintable insults and shook angry fists in each others' faces. Hundreds of experts concocted thousands of remedies. None worked.

Meanwhile, a confused young artist, Benoit Raclet, was having his own troubles at Moulin à Vent. Since his paintings brought hardly enough to pay for new brushes, he depended on a pocket-sized vineyard for support. But he had just married, and his wife's housekeeping habits were driving him to desperation. Instead of treating the noble vines with the tender consideration expected of a *vigneron's* mate, she would carelessly slosh the scalding dishwater right out the kitchen window, splashing it midleaf on the nearest plants. What laziness! What sacrilege! *Quelle femme!* Despite Benoit's pleadings and protests, despite a mother-in-law's waspish

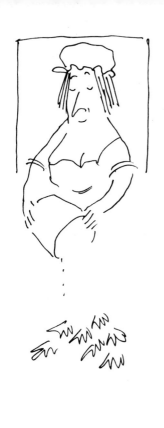

scoldings, his bride yielded not a millimeter in refusing to lug heavy pails to the backyard.

When robins trilling in the poplars announced Spring, Benoit made a perplexing discovery. The dreaded *pyrales*, emerging from their cocoon hibernation with the accumulated appetite of months of fast, were greedily gobbling wine leaves from one end of Beaujolais to another, stripping each stalk to a skeleton. His own mournful vineyard looked bare as barbed wire—except for a defiant little clump of vines that remained luxuriantly leafy—those which Madame had scalded.

Next winter, Benoit, ceaselessly reproached his wife for not having scalded the entire vineyard, dashed back and forth from kitchen to vine-row, a boiling kettle swinging from each hand. When May arrived and insect disaster again assailed his neighbors, Raclet's vineyard glistened with grapes—a glimmering oasis of green health in a desert of disease.

Gossip of the miraculous, hot-dishwater treatment sizzled through France. Beaune and Bordeaux, Sancerre and St. Estèphe rushed to try Benoit's strategy—some vintners even venturing to use ordinary hot water instead of hot dishwater. Everywhere, success! Nowadays, when March arrives on the calendar pad, giant cauldrons bubble in the winefields, vineyard volcanoes shooting up white puffs of steam to signal that the grape-harvest is going to be good. Was there ever more convincing triumph for woman's instinct?